VIN C. BU

200

DELIVERANCE PRAYERS AGAINST WITCHCRAFT OPERATIONS, MANIPULATION, AND EVIL SPELL

Destroying witchcraft operations Totally

Vin C. Butcher

Copyright © Vin C. Butcher 2017

All rights reserved

No part of this work should be used in any way without the written permission of the publisher

E-mail: vincentbutcher@gmail.com

Unless otherwise indicated, all Scripture quotations are taken from the King James Version of the Holy Bible.

TABLE OF CONTENTS

TABLE OF CONTENT...3

HOW TO USE THIS BOOK............................4

INTRODUCTION...,,6

PRAYER BULLETS..9

OTHER BOOKS BY THE AUTHOR

1. 200 Deliverance Prayer Against Witchcraft Operations, Manipulation And Evil Spell: Destroying Witchcraft Operation Totally

2. 162 Prayer Bullets For Deliverance: Prayer That Guarantees Deliverance From The Strongman

3. 315 Prayer Bullets That Guarantees All Round Breakthrough: Prayer That Dismantles Satanic Spells, Destroys Witchcraft Manipulations And Guarantees All Round Breakthrough

4. **Command The Day: Daily Devotional, Prophetic Declarations, Prayer Bullets, And Daily Bible Study Plan**

HOW TO USE THIS BOOK

These prayer bullets are effective when used by a child of God. You must know that it is not everybody on the earth that are children of God. Being a child of God is by choice.

'Ye are of your father the devil, and the lusts of your father ye will do. he was a murderer from the beginning, and abide not in the truth, because there is no truth in him. When he speaketh a lie, he speaks of his own: for he is a liar, and the father of it.'
John 8:44

As I have said, being a child of God is by choice and not automatic. So I want to lead you to Christ before we proceed in praying these dangerous praeyrs, so that this prayer bullets will be a blessing to you and not a curse.

'The sacrifice of the wicked is an

abomination to the LORD: but the prayer of the upright is his delight.

9 The way of the wicked is an abomination unto the LORD: but he loveth him that followeth after righteousness.' Pro 15:8

If you pray these prayers as a sinner, it will be an abomination to the ears of God, and will not yield any result, but when prayed as a Child of God, it will scatter the kingdom of darkness, scatter the covens of witches and wizards, and release your caged blessings.

Pray this prayer to receive Jesus Christ into your life.

Say after me,

Lord Jesus, I come to you as a sinner. I know I am a sinner that can't help myself. I give my life to you, wash me with the blood of Jesus Christ, give me the power to become a child of God. Thank you for doing it.

These prayer bullets will be more effective in the night period, because the kingdom of darkness perpetuate havoc on mankind mostly in the night.

'Another parable put he forth unto them, saying, The kingdom of heaven is likened unto a man who sowed good seed in his field:

But while men slept, his enemy came and sowed tares among the wheat, and went his way.' Matt 13:24

Most demonic atrocities, calamities are perpetuated in the night period. Pause and ponder on this. Why do most attacks on humanity happen in the night? According to the above scripture, it is when men sleeps that the devil (the enemy) attacks.

Many have woken up with incurable diseases, sickness, madness. Many have slept as wealthy, but woken up and loose all their fortune overnight mysteriously, due to the operations of the kingdom of darkness in the night.

This prayer bullet is meant to scatter whatever the enemies have done against you, your family, your business etc.

Start this prayer by midnight and pray it for a minimum of two hours for seven days.

Start with singing praise and worship songs, because it brings down the presence of God. Sing for at least for 45 minutes.

Begin to thank God for His goodness, call Him sweet names as you are led of the Holy Spirit.

Pray for mercy for yourself and your family using Psalm 51

Invite the presence of the Holy Spirit and the Angels of God to surround you and your house..

Pray against the spirit of fear.

Then, start praying with the prayer bullet with holy anger in your spirit, pray with desperation.

Pray each prayer bullet for at least 5mins

Use only ten prayer bullets per session

The prayer bullets can be repeated because the potency doesn't expire.

INTRODUCTION

This book is a compilation of proven, and result oriented prayer bullets that will guarantee your freedom from the dominion of the powers of darkness, and guarantee your freedom.

The disciples of Jesus asked Him.

'And it came to pass, that, as He was praying in a certain place, when he ceased, one of his disciples said unto Him, Lord, teach us to pray, as John also taught his disciples.

And he said unto them, When you pray, say, Our Father which art in heaven, Hallowed be thy name. Thy kingdom come. Thy will be done, as in heaven, so in earth.' Luke 11:1-2

Jesus also gave a prayer guide to His disciples, which we call today 'The Lord's prayer.' He gave them a guide on how to pray.

This book is to give you a guide on how to fight against the powers of darkness that attacks you through many mediums.

Obad.1:3-4, Nahum 3:1-4;

The pride of your heart has deceived thee, thou that dwellest in the clefts of the rock, whose habitation is high: that saith in his heart, who shall bring me down to the ground? Though thou exalt thyself as the eagle, and though thou set thy nest among the stars, thence will I bring thee down, saith the Lord.

Ezek. 11:2-3, 7, 11:

Which say, It is not near; let us build houses: this city is the caldron, and we be the flesh.. Therefore thus saith the Lord God; your slain which ye have laid in the midst of it, they are the flesh, and this city is the caldron: but I will bring you forth out of the midst of it.

Mal.3:3:

Who also eat the flesh of my people and flay their skin from off them; and they break their bones and chop them in pieces, as for the pot, and as flesh within the caldron. Cover yourself with the blood of Jesus. You do not go into battle with them without covering yourself with the Blood of Jesus.

PRAYER BULLETS

1. I plead the blood of Jesus Christ over this environment. Always cover the environment with the Blood of Jesus Christ, in the mighty name of our Lord Jesus Christ.

2. I reject every involvement of the flesh and Satan in my prayers. The flesh is a friend to witchcraft in the mighty name of our Lord Jesus Christ.

3. I call on the God of Heavens- O God, rend the heavens in your anger come down into this territory and make your presence known in the mighty name of our Lord Jesus Christ.

4. My heavenly Father, let every witchcraft covens where my name is called melt away as wax before fire in the mighty name of our Lord Jesus Christ.

5. Oh Lord God, arise and destroy all witchcraft incantations made agaisnt me with thunder,

earthquake and a great noise in the mighty name of our Lord Jesus Christ.

6. O God arise and instruct your angels to set unquenchable fires on all witchcraft shrines or habitation militating against me in the mighty name of our Lord Jesus Christ.

7. Oh Lord God, arise and cause confusion in witchcraft camps assigned against me in the mighty name of our Lord Jesus Christ.

8. I call for protocol angels, battle angels, security angels, ministering angels, territorial angels to slay every power of witchcraft working in my foundation in the mighty name of our Lord Jesus Christ.

9. Oh! thou Earth, refuse to carry out the instructions of witch doctors, witches and wizards assigned against me in the mighty name of our Lord Jesus Christ.

10. I deprogramme and cancel all witchcraft prophecies by the power in the blood of Jesus Christ in the mighty name of our Lord Jesus Christ.

11. I programme judgment on every witchcraft formation working against me in the heavenlies in the mighty name of our Lord Jesus Christ.

12. Oh Lord God arise and cast abominable filth upon witchcraft powers programmed agaisnt me in the mighty name of our Lord Jesus Christ.

13. My Father let the tables of witchcraft become their snares in the mighty name of our Lord Jesus Christ.

14. I command that every human blood will become a snare to them so that if they ever move close to any human blood, they will get into trouble in the mighty name of our Lord Jesus Christ.

15. Oh Lord God Let the eyes of the witches assigned against me be darkened in the mighty name of our Lord Jesus Christ.

16. Let the covens of witches become desolate so that none can dwell in them in the mighty name of our Lord Jesus Christ.

17. Let every witchcraft power flying against me crash-land in the mighty name of our Lord Jesus Christ.

18. I decree that no witch or wizard can prosper in my environment in the mighty name of our Lord Jesus Christ.

19. I command every water spirit that is networking with witchcraft spirit against my life to be judged by fire in the mighty name of our Lord Jesus Christ.

20. Every queen of heaven that is networking with witchcraft to fight me, I judge you by fire.

21. I command the sun go down on witchcraft power in the mighty name of our Lord Jesus Christ.

22. I command the days of witches and wizards to be dark in the mighty name of our Lord Jesus Christ.

23. Oh Lord, my God, Let the sun smite them by day, and the moon smite by night in the mighty name of our Lord Jesus Christ.

24. Let the stars in the courses fight against witches or wizards in the mighty name of our Lord Jesus Christ.

25. I shut down all witchcraft buildings with the key of David in the mighty name of our Lord Jesus Christ.

26. Oh Lord God arise and send down your whirlwind with great pain upon the heads of witchcraft in the mighty name of our Lord Jesus Christ.

27. O God arise and trample down every witchcraft company in the mighty name of our Lord Jesus Christ.

28. O God arise and cause stormy winds to fall upon witchcraft powers in the mighty name of our Lord Jesus Christ.

29. O God arise and bring upon the army of witchcraft the day of disasters in the mighty name of our Lord Jesus Christ.

30. Every spell and enchantment of witchcraft clear off in the name of Jesus in the mighty name of our Lord Jesus Christ.

31. Every agenda of witchcraft over my family I cut you off in the mighty name of our Lord Jesus Christ.

32. Witchcraft in the water, I crush your power in the mighty name of our Lord Jesus Christ.

33. Witchcraft agenda for my destiny I destroy you in the mighty name of our Lord Jesus Christ.

34. Every witchcraft power assigned to convert my life destiny to the dustbin, I dislodge your power in the mighty name of our Lord Jesus Christ.

35. Oh Lord my God every Witchcraft assigned to resurrect affliction, die by fire in the mighty name of our Lord Jesus Christ.

36. Witchcraft game plan over my success I destroy you in the mighty name of our Lord Jesus Christ.

37. Every yoke manufactured by witchcraft to attack my life catch your owner now in the mighty name of our Lord Jesus Christ.

38. Oh Lord my God let every pregnancy of sorrow assigned against my breakthrough by witchcraft power I abort you now in the mighty name of our Lord Jesus Christ.

39. I upset every witchcraft set up against my life in the mighty name of our Lord Jesus Christ.

40. I break every witchcraft imprisonment over my life in the mighty name of our Lord Jesus Christ.

41. Let every witchcraft remote control against my life I black you out in the mighty name of our Lord Jesus Christ.

42. Witchcraft powers sponsoring repeated problems in my life, carry your problems in the mighty name of our Lord Jesus Christ.

43. I speak destruction unto every occultic assignment against me in the mighty name of our Lord Jesus Christ.

44. Every household witchcraft assigned to waste my life, be wasted in the mighty name of our Lord Jesus Christ.

45. Witchcraft altars, priests, die in the mighty name of our Lord Jesus Christ.

46. Every yoke designed by marine powers against my life, break in the mighty name of our Lord Jesus Christ.

47. Oh Lord my God, every evil load of witchcraft, go back to your senders in the mighty name of our Lord Jesus Christ.

48. Every witchcraft prayers against my life, scatter in the mighty name of our Lord Jesus Christ.

49. Every environmental witchcraft, in the mighty name of our Lord Jesus Christ.

50. Every witchcraft grip on my life/family be dismantled in the mighty name of our Lord Jesus Christ. in the mighty name of our Lord Jesus Christ.

51. Oh Lord god let the thunder of God locate and dismantle the throne of witchcraft in my household, in the mighty name of our Lord Jesus Christ.

52. My father my Father let every seat of witchcraft in my household be roasted with the fire of God, in the mighty name of our Lord Jesus Christ.

53. Oh Lord God let the altar of witchcraft in my household be roasted, in the mighty name of our Lord Jesus Christ.

54. Let the thunder of God scatter beyond redemption the foundation of witchcraft in my household, in the mighty name of our Lord Jesus Christ.

55. Every stronghold or refuge of my household witches, be destroyed, in the mighty name of our Lord Jesus Christ.

56. Oh Lord my God every hiding place and secret place of witchcraft in my family, be exposed by fire, in the mighty name of our Lord Jesus Christ.

57. Let every local and international witchcraft network of my household witches be shattered to pieces, in the mighty name of our Lord Jesus Christ.

58. Oh Lord my God let the communication system of my household witches be frustrated, in the mighty name of our Lord Jesus Christ.

59. Let the terrible fire of God consume the transportation of my household witchcraft, in the mighty name of our Lord Jesus Christ.

60. I command thate very agent ministering at the altar of witchcraft in my household, fall down and die, in the mighty name of our Lord Jesus Christ.

61. Oh Lord my God let the thunder and the fire of God locate the storehouses and strong rooms of my household witchcraft harboring my blessings and pull them down in the mighty name of Jesus Christ.

62. Let every witchcraft curse working against me be revoked by the blood of Jesus Christ in the mighty name of our Lord Jesus Christ.

63. Oh Lord my God every decision, vow and covenant of household witchcraft affecting me, be nullified by the blood of Jesus Christ in the mighty name of our Lord Jesus Christ.

64. I destroy with the fire of God, every weapon of witchcraft used against me, in the mighty name of our Lord Jesus Christ.

65. Oh Lord my God any material taken from my body and placed on witchcraft altar, be roasted by the fire of God, in the mighty name of our Lord Jesus Christ.

66. I reverse every witchcraft burial fashioned against me, in the mighty name of our Lord Jesus Christ.

67. My Father my Father, I command that every trap set for me by witches begin to catch your owners, in the mighty name of our Lord Jesus Christ.

68. Oh Lord my God every witchcraft padlock fashioned against any area of my life be roasted, in the mighty name of our Lord Jesus Christ.

69. Let the wisdom of my household witches be converted to foolishness, in the mighty name of our Lord Jesus Christ.

70. Oh Lord let the wickedness of my household enemies overturn them, in the mighty name of our Lord Jesus Christ.

71. Oh Lord my God I deliver my soul from every witchcraft bewitchment, in the mighty name of our Lord Jesus Christ.

72. Any witchcraft bird flying for my sake, fall down and die and be roasted to ashes, in the mighty name of our Lord Jesus Christ.

73. Oh Lord my God Oh Lord my God, any of my blessing, traded out by household witches be returned to me, in the mighty name of our Lord Jesus Christ.

74. My Father my Father any of my blessings and testimonies swallowed by witches, be converted to hot coals of fire of God and be vomited, in the mighty name of our Lord Jesus Christ.

75. Oh Lord my God I break myself loose from every bondage of witchcraft covenant, in the mighty name of our Lord Jesus Christ.

76. My Father my Father any witchcraft coven where any of my blessings are hidden, be roasted by the fire of God, in the mighty name of our Lord Jesus Christ.

77. My Father my Father, I command every witchcraft spirit plantation, pollution, deposits and

materials operating in my body to be melted by the fire of God and be flushed out by the blood of Jesus Christ in the mighty name of our Lord Jesus Christ.

78. Oh Lord my God every evil ever done to me through witchcraft attack, be reversed, in the mighty name of our Lord Jesus Christ.

79. Every damage done to my destiny through witchcraft operations, be reversed now, in the mighty name of our Lord Jesus Christ.

80. Every witchcraft man planting evil seeds in my life through dream attacks, wither and burn to ashes, in the mighty name of our Lord Jesus Christ.

81. Oh Lord my God every witchcraft obstacle and hindrance put on the road to my desired miracle and success, be removed by the East wind of God, in the mighty name of our Lord Jesus Christ.

82. Every witchcraft chants, spells and projections made against me, I bind you and turn you against your owner, in the mighty name of our Lord Jesus Christ.

83. My Father my Father I frustrate every plot, device, scheme, and projects of witchcraft designed to affect any area of my life, in the mighty name of our Lord Jesus Christ.

84. Oh Lord my God, any witch, projecting into the blood of any animal in order to do me harm or evil, be trapped in the body of such an animal forever, in the mighty name of our Lord Jesus Christ.

85. My Father my Father any drop of my blood sucked by any witch, be vomited now, in the mighty name of our Lord Jesus Christ.

86. My Father my Father, any part of me given out amongst household and village witches, I recover you, in the name of our Lord Jesus Christ.

87. I command that any organ of my body that has been exchanged for another one through witchcraft operations, be replaced now, in the mighty name of our Lord Jesus Christ.

88. I recover any of my virtues/blessings shared out amongst village/household witches, in the mighty name of our Lord Jesus Christ.

89. I reverse the evil effect of any witchcraft invocation or summoning of my spirit, in the mighty name of our Lord Jesus Christ.

90. My Father my Father, I lose my hands and feet from any witchcraft bewitchment and bondage, in the mighty name of our Lord Jesus Christ.

91. Let the blood of Jesus wash away every witchcraft identification mark on me or on any of my property, in the mighty name of our Lord Jesus Christ.

92. I forbid any reunion or re-gathering of household and village witches against my life, in the mighty name of our Lord Jesus Christ.

93. Let the entire body system of my household witches be upset until they confess all their wickedness, in the mighty name of our Lord Jesus Christ.

94. Let the mercies of God be withdrawn from them in the mighty name of our Lord Jesus Christ.

95. Let them begin to grope in the daytime as in the thickness of a dark night, in the mighty name of our Lord Jesus Christ.

96. Let everything that has ever worked for the kingdom of darkness begin to work against them, in the mighty name of our Lord Jesus Christ.

97. Let them not have a cloth to cover their shame, in the mighty name of our Lord Jesus Christ.

98. Let as many of them as are stubbornly unrepentant be smitten by the sun in the day and by the moon at night, in the mighty name of our Lord Jesus Christ.

99. Let each step they take lead them to greater destruction, in the mighty name of our Lord Jesus Christ.

100. But as for me, let me dwell in the hollow of God's hand, in the mighty name of our Lord Jesus Christ.

101. I command that the goodness and mercies of God now overwhelm me, in the mighty name of our Lord Jesus Christ.

102. I force feed witchcraft powers with their own blood, in the mighty name of our Lord Jesus Christ.

103. Every foundation of witchcraft in my household, be smashed by the Rock of ages, in the mighty name of our Lord Jesus Christ.

104. Every seat of witchcraft, receive the thunder fire of God, in the mighty name of our Lord Jesus Christ.

105. Every habitation of witchcraft, be scattered unto desolation, in the mighty name of our Lord Jesus Christ.

106. Every throne of witchcraft, be dismantled by fire, in the mighty name of our Lord Jesus Christ.

107. Every stronghold of witchcraft in my life, receive divine acid, in the mighty name of our Lord Jesus Christ.

108. Let the witchcraft network be shattered to pieces, in the mighty name of our Lord Jesus Christ.

109. Let their communication system be damaged by fire, in the mighty name of our Lord Jesus Christ.

110. Every stubborn and unrepentant witchcraft, be exposed and disgraced, in the mighty name of our Lord Jesus Christ.

111. Let their hiding place be dissolved by fire, in the mighty name of our Lord Jesus Christ.

112. Let their transportation system scattered to pieces, in the mighty name of our Lord Jesus Christ.

113. I withdraw my blessings from every witchcraft storehouse and strong room, in the mighty name of our Lord Jesus Christ.

114. Let every witchcraft curse go back to the sender sevenfold, in the mighty name of our Lord Jesus Christ.

115. Every covenant of witchcraft, be melted by the blood of Jesus Christ, in the mighty name of our Lord Jesus Christ.

116. Every weapon of witchcraft, turn against your users, in the mighty name of our Lord Jesus Christ.

117. I reverse every witchcraft burial fashioned against me, in the mighty name of our Lord Jesus Christ.

118. As I begin to pray, I withdraw every organ of my body from any witchcraft altar, in the mighty name of our Lord Jesus Christ.

119. Every trap of witchcraft, catch your owners, in the mighty name of our Lord Jesus Christ.

120. Every witchcraft padlock fashioned against me, be roasted, in the mighty name of our Lord Jesus Christ.

121. I deliver my soul from every witchcraft bewitchment, in the mighty name of our Lord Jesus Christ.

122. Every damage done to my destiny by witchcraft, be reversed, in the mighty name of our Lord Jesus Christ.

123. Every witchcraft utterance and projections made against me, be overthrown, in the mighty name of our Lord Jesus Christ.

124. Any drop of my blood sucked by any witch, be vomited now, in the mighty name of our Lord Jesus Christ.

125. I reverse the effect of every witchcraft summoning of my spirit, in the mighty name of our Lord Jesus Christ.

126. Every witchcraft identification mark, be wipe off by the blood of Jesus Christ in the mighty name of our Lord Jesus Christ.

127.   I frustrate every witchcraft exchange of my virtues, in the mighty name of our Lord Jesus Christ.

128.   As I begin to pray, I command that anything planted in my life by witchcraft, come out now, in the mighty name of our Lord Jesus Christ.

129.   Let each step taken by witchcraft against me lead them to greater destruction, in the mighty name of our Lord Jesus Christ.

130.   I declare my environment and my house no-flying zone for witchcraft birds, in the mighty name of our Lord Jesus Christ.

131.   As I begin to pray, I cut off the roots of witchcraft in the water, in the mighty name of our Lord Jesus Christ.

132.   Anything deposited in my life by marine witchcraft, come out now, in the mighty name of our Lord Jesus Christ.

133. Anything deposited in my life by household witchcraft, come out now, in the mighty name of our Lord Jesus Christ.

134. My Father my Father, I take authority over this year, in the mighty name of our Lord Jesus Christ.

135. My Father my Father, I decree that all elements of this year will cooperate with me, in the mighty name of our Lord Jesus Christ.

136. I decree that these elemental forces will refuse to cooperate with my enemies this year, in the mighty name of our Lord Jesus Christ.

137. I speak unto the sun, the moon and the stars, they will not smite my family and me this year, in the mighty name of our Lord Jesus Christ.

138. I pull down every contrary energy planning to operate against my life this year, in the mighty name of our Lord Jesus Christ.

139. My Father my Father, I confess that this is the year the Lord has made and I will rejoice and be glad in it, in the mighty name of our Lord Jesus Christ.

140. I dismantle any power that is uttering incantations to capture this year, in the mighty name of our Lord Jesus Christ.

141. I render such incantations and satanic prayer null and void over my family and me, in the mighty name of our Lord Jesus Christ.

142. My Father my Father, as I begin to pray I retrieve this year out of their hands, in the mighty name of our Lord Jesus Christ.

143. Spirits of favor, counsel, might and power, come upon me, in the mighty name of our Lord Jesus Christ.

144. I shall excel this year, and nothing shall defile me, in the mighty name of our Lord Jesus Christ.

145. My Father my Father, I command that I shall possess the gates of my enemies this year, in the mighty name of our Lord Jesus Christ.

146. I decree that the Lord shall anoint me with the oil of gladness above my fellows this year, in the mighty name of our Lord Jesus Christ.

147. The fire of the enemy will not burn my family and me this year, in the mighty name of our Lord Jesus Christ.

148. My ears shall hear good news, and I shall not hear the voice of the enemy, in the mighty name of our Lord Jesus Christ.

149. I decree that my life and the lives of the members of my family are secured in Christ, in the mighty name of our Lord Jesus Christ.

150. Let every satanic check-point mounted against me in the heavenlies be dismantled by the word of the Lord, in the mighty name of our Lord Jesus Christ.

151. Every evil altar prepared against my breakthroughs in the heavenlies, and in the sea, be dismantled by fire, in the mighty name of our Lord Jesus Christ.

152. Every arrangement that sorceries and witches have prepared against me be overthrown, in the mighty name of our Lord Jesus Christ.

153. Any evil thing programmed into the sun and moon against my life, be dismantled, in the mighty name of our Lord Jesus Christ.

154. I command you spiritual wickedness in the heavenlies fighting against my star, I bring the hook of the Lord against you and frustrate your activities, in the mighty name of our Lord Jesus Christ.

155. I receive open heavens for my life this year, in the mighty name of our Lord Jesus Christ.

156. I take divine insurance against all forms of accident and tragedy, in the mighty name of our Lord Jesus Christ.

157. I send lightning, thunder and the hook of the Lord against the evil queen in the heavenlies militating against me, in the mighty name of our Lord Jesus Christ.

158. Every evil spiritual-equation programmed against my life, I command you to change, in the mighty name of our Lord Jesus Christ.

159. I speak unto my umbilical gate to overthrow every negative parental spirit, in the mighty name of our Lord Jesus Christ.

160. I break the yoke of any evil spirit having access to any organ in my body, in the mighty name of our Lord Jesus Christ.

161. I speak unto the headquarters of evil programmers and blow up their altars, in the mighty name of our Lord Jesus Christ.

162. Any evil thing written in the cycle of the moon against me, be blotted out, in the mighty name of our Lord Jesus Christ.

163. My Father my Father, I command the siege of the enemy against my life to be dismantled in the mighty name of our Lord Jesus Christ.

164. I come by faith to Mount Zion, and I command deliverance upon my life, in the mighty name of our Lord Jesus Christ.

165. I file a counter report in heaven against any dark spirit militating against me, in the mighty name of our Lord Jesus Christ.

166. My Father my Father, I bring the blood of Jesus over the stubborn pursuer that does not want me to go, in the mighty name of our Lord Jesus Christ.

167. I bring the blood of Jesus over every evidence that can be tendered by wicked spirit against me, in the mighty name of our Lord Jesus Christ.

168. I announce to the heavenlies that I am married to Jesus Christ, in the mighty name of our Lord Jesus Christ.

169. Every evil handwriting engraved by demonic iron pen against me, be wiped off by the blood of Jesus Christ, in the mighty name of our Lord Jesus Christ.

170. Praise the Lord for the power in His name at which every knee must bow, in the mighty name of our Lord Jesus Christ.

171. Every wicked pot cooking my affairs, be roasted, in the mighty name of our Lord Jesus Christ.

172. Every witchcraft pot working against me, I bring the judgment of God against you, in the mighty name of our Lord Jesus Christ.

173. My place of birth will not be my caldron, in the mighty name of our Lord Jesus Christ.

174. This city where I live, will not be my boiler, in the mighty name of our Lord Jesus Christ.

175. Every pot of darkness seated against my life, be destroyed by fire, in the mighty name of our Lord Jesus Christ.

176. I command every witchcraft pot using remote control against my heath to be broken into pieces, in the mighty name of our Lord Jesus Christ.

177. Every power calling my name into any caldrons, fall down and die, in the mighty name of our Lord Jesus Christ.

178. Every caldron making noise against me and monitoring my life, disintegrate, in the mighty name of our Lord Jesus Christ.

179. Every power cooking my progress in an evil pot, receive the fire of judgment, in the mighty name of our Lord Jesus Christ.

180. Every satanic programme emanating from the caldron of darkness, be reversed, in the mighty name of our Lord Jesus Christ.

181. Any evil fire boiling any satanic porgramme in my life, be quenched, in the mighty name of our Lord Jesus Christ.

182. My Father my Father, I command the counsel of the wicked against my life in this city shall not stand, and I command them to perish, in the mighty name of our Lord Jesus Christ.

183. Let the counsel of God for my life prosper, in the mighty name of our Lord Jesus Christ.

184. Every evil power cooking my flesh and my health in any evil caldron, receive the fire of God, in the mighty name of our Lord Jesus Christ.

185. Every evil bird of satanic programme emanating from any caldron of darkness, fall down and die, in the mighty name of our Lord Jesus Christ.

186. Every pot cooking my affairs, the Lord rebuke you, in the mighty name of our Lord Jesus Christ.

187. I rebuke the spell of any witchcraft pot over my life, in the mighty name of our Lord Jesus Christ.

188. I break every witchcraft pot over my life, in the mighty name of our Lord Jesus Christ.

189. Let every evil pot hunt their owners, in the mighty name of our Lord Jesus Christ.

190. I release my life from your caldron of mischief planners, blood polluters, envious witchcraft, destiny killers, health destroyers, priests operating on evil altars, in the mighty name of our Lord Jesus Christ.

191. I release my life from your caldron of blood hunters, eaters of flesh and drinkers of blood, household witchcraft, star hunters, in the mighty name of our Lord Jesus Christ.

192. Every evil caldron or pot, be judged from heaven, in the mighty name of our Lord Jesus Christ.

193. No evil caldron will cook up my life, in the mighty name of our Lord Jesus Christ.

194. Every council of witchcraft working against me will not prosper, in the mighty name of our Lord Jesus Christ.

195. Every agreement with Satan over my life, I cancel you now, in the mighty name of our Lord Jesus Christ.

196. Every astral projection against me, I frustrate you, in the mighty name of our Lord Jesus Christ.

197. I disentangle myself and my family from every witchcraft cage and pot, in the mighty name of our Lord Jesus Christ.

198. Every enemy that will not let go quickly, I bring the judgment of death against you, in the mighty name of our Lord Jesus Christ.

199. This year, my blessings will not sink, in the mighty name of our Lord Jesus Christ.

200.	Let the spirit of salvation fall upon my family, in the mighty name of our Lord Jesus Christ.

Begin to thank God for answering your prayers. Sing some praise songs.

OTHER BOOKS BY THE AUTHOR

1. 200 Deliverance Prayer Against Witchcraft Operations, Manipulation And Evil Spell: Destroying Witchcraft Operation Totally

2. 162 Prayer Bullets For Deliverance: Prayer That Guarantees Deliverance From The Strongman

3. 315 Prayer Bullets That Guarantees All Round Breakthrough: Prayer That Dismantles Satanic Spells, Destroys Witchcraft Manipulations And Guarantees All Round Breakthrough

4. **Command The Day: Daily Devotional, Prophetic Declarations, Prayer Bullets, And Daily Bible Study Plan**

Made in United States
Troutdale, OR
09/01/2024

22511422R00031